THE HOUSES OF MARTHA'S VINEYARD

Keith Moskow

THE HOUSES OF MARTHA'S VINEYARD

The Monacelli Press

For Allison, Zack, and Jake

First published in the
United States of America in 2005 by
The Monacelli Press
611 Broadway, New York, New York 10012

Library of Congress Cataloging-in-Publication Data

Moskow, Keith.
The houses of Martha's Vineyard / Keith Moskow.
p. cm.
ISBN 1-58093-153-7
1. Architecture, Domestic—Massachusetts—Martha's Vineyard.
2. Architecture—Massachusetts—Martha's Vineyard—20th century. 3.
Architecture—Massachusetts—Martha's Vineyard—21st century. I. Title.
NA7235.M42M375 2005
728'.37'0974494–dc22   2004017318

Front cover: Robert A. M. Stern Architects, Chilmark Residence
Back cover: Steven Holl Architects, Berkowitz-Odgis House
             Charles Rose, Vineyard Sound Residence

Printed and bound in Italy
Book and jacket design by Paul G. Wagner

CONTENTS

INTRODUCTION
MARTHA'S VINEYARD—PAST & PRESENT

JUST OFF THE COAST OF CAPE COD, MARTHA'S VINEYARD HAS CAPTURED THE public's imagination as an idyllic summer destination. Home to fishermen and farmers for centuries, the island has, over the past thirty years, become a flourishing summer retreat, with a population that swells to over 100,000 during the summer and draws celebrities, presidential entourages, and many tourists and part-time residents. They come to enjoy the beaches, grasslands, moors, pine forests, picturesque New England towns, and historic sites that document the island's rich past. In recent years, a constellation of remarkable architects, both emerging and internationally renowned, have designed houses that respond to the Vineyard's unique context and in many instances represent their best work.

As a lifelong summer and occasional full-time resident, I have watched the island evolve. Strict zoning and strong conservation initiatives—32 percent of the island is protected from development—have curtailed multistory hotels, strip malls, and subdivisions, thus preserving much of the island's original character. At the same time, many contemporary architects have achieved high standards of building and devised creative responses to the Vineyard's varied landscape and densely layered social and historical context.

The Houses of Martha's Vineyard highlights the island's recent architectural achievements, singling out twenty-four houses that work successfully in this rich and diverse environment. For instance, when designing a house perched over the Atlantic Ocean, Steven Holl found inspiration in the island's whaling history and literary past: in *Moby Dick*, Herman Melville describes how Native Americans move the skeleton of a beached whale to dry land, stretch dried skins over it, and transform it into a home. Like the Indians' shelter, Holl's house acknowledges the living record of the whale, putting the weathered gray "bones" of the wooden frame on the exterior while situating the contemporary domicile, complete with master suite and exercise center, in the belly.

Another example of innovative design that draws on the island's context is Margaret McCurry's Lighthouse, set in a wooded thicket among turn-of-the-century Shingle Style manses in West Chop. She contemporizes the traditional design features with new twists and incorporates figurative iconography—specifically West Chop Light—in the facade.

Margaret McCurry Architects, The Lighthouse, 1993.

Topography

Martha's Vineyard is roughly triangular, with maximum distances of approximately twenty miles east to west and ten miles north to south. The west end of the island, referred to as up-island (from the nautical expression of going "up" in degrees of longitude as you sail west) remains fairly rural and is characterized by the rolling moors and multicolored cliffs of the Wampanoag tribal lands. The eastern end of the Vineyard (down-island) is more urban, featuring the three most populated towns: Vineyard Haven, Oak Bluffs, and Edgartown.

Martha's Vineyard's diverse geography—farmland, forests, moors, cranberry bogs, sandy beaches and dunes, craggy oceanfront—is largely the result of two glacial moraines that came to rest at the end of the last ice age. In the intervening centuries, the ocean molded the shore while different groups of inhabitants left their imprint on the land. Much of the upland moor that characterizes Chilmark and Aquinnah, for example, is the result of the sheep farming that was the islanders' principal occupation during the eighteenth and early nineteenth centuries. At that time, moors spanned the entire island. In recent years, many of these moors have been allowed to return to their natural forested state. As such, the "natural" beauty of Martha's Vineyard evolves with human influences.[1]

History

The first residents of Martha's Vineyard were Wampanoag Indians, and some of their descendants still live in the town of Aquinnah. Their earliest camps, which were recently excavated, have been carbon-dated to 2270 B.C. The first Europeans arrived in 1602, when Bartholomew Gosnold charted Martha's Vineyard for the British Crown. He named the island after his daughter and after the wild grapes that blanketed the land. At the time of Gosnold's arrival, there were approximately three thousand Native Americans living in four main tribes on the island. However, as in much of the New World, diseases brought by the English decimated the native population. The first white settlers arrived in the mid-1600s, and for the next 150 years they and their offspring lived isolated lives, fishing and farming.

Shortly after 1800, residents of the Vineyard, already skillful seamen, began to embark on extended whaling voyages. Although never as predominant in the industry as Nantucket or New Bedford, Martha's Vineyard nevertheless garnered its share of the enormous profits. The prosperous whaling captains built mansions along the streets of Edgartown and Vineyard Haven. But by 1871, the whaling industry had collapsed, and Vineyarders reverted to fishing and farming as they cast about for new ways to make a living.

The Vineyard's development as a summer resort began with the Methodist Camp Meetings. In 1835 Vineyarders left their houses in Edgartown for a week of group worship in the wilderness of what would become Oak Bluffs. By 1857 the original 9 tents had multiplied to 250, and visitors from New York and Boston flocked to the area. Before long, permanent platforms were erected, and over time cottages in the Carpenter Gothic style began to appear and Oak Bluffs was established as a town. The nature of these pilgrimages shifted as well, from religious retreats to recreation. African Americans were particularly well represented among the worshipers, and Oak Bluffs is considered by many to be America's original African-American summer retreat.

Despite its popularity as a summer destination, the Vineyard was slow to build first-class hotels or improve roads, and it made no recreational use of its harbors. Summer business withered in the wake of every stock market crash or recession. In the late nineteenth century and the first half of the twentieth century, summer residents came to enjoy the simple life—the only kind Martha's Vineyard offered. Given its proximity to New York and Boston, however, the Vineyard couldn't escape attention forever.

The year-round population of fifteen thousand residents grows sixfold in the summer, with an additional twenty-five thousand day-trippers arriving by ferry each day. The pressures on the Vineyard to conform to mainland standards of pace, comfort, entertainment, and appearance are constant, and preservation groups fight against forces of change that would alter the island's original character.[2]

From left to right: Vincent House, 1672; Oak Bluffs cottages; houses in Edgartown; Eliot Noyes House; Hugh Jacobsen House; Chet Wisniewski House.

Architectural History

The architecture of Martha's Vineyard reflects its colonial history, its economic success during the whaling era, and its emergence as a popular resort. The first English settlers built simple homes—one-story wood-and-shingle structures in keeping with both their Puritan beliefs and the challenges of island living. One example is the Vincent House (1672) in Edgartown, the oldest house on the Vineyard, occupied by the same family for 250 years until it became a museum. As time passed, second stories were added to Capes, creating colonial houses such as the Thomas Cooke House (1765), also in Edgartown. The Vineyard had almost no saltbox houses until the late twentieth century, when developers built them, assuming they represented the historical style of the island.

Classically inspired architecture came to the Vineyard during the nineteenth century, when whaling captains and investors vied with one another to demonstrate their success through the grandeur of their homes. Examples of their efforts are found primarily in Edgartown.

The houses in Oak Bluffs, formerly the site of the Methodist Camp Meetings, are in a very different style: John Wesley, the founder of Methodism, sought a more loving, personal approach to God, and the spontaneity of his approach is reflected in Oak Bluffs' cottages, which reject both the chaste elegance of the Classical Revival period and the heavy Victorian style. These cottages, which replaced the original tents after the Civil War, were built in the Carpenter Gothic style and have distinctive gingerbread trim.

The early twentieth century saw the development of large Shingle Style summer homes found in East and West Chop and on the waterfront around the island. They were built by wealthy off-islanders who wanted to experience a simple, rustic existence on the Vineyard.[3]

Contemporary Architecture

Contemporary architecture made its way to the Vineyard in the 1960s, before the island became a major tourist destination. Families from New England and New York who chose the island as a summer destination eventually began to purchase property and build summer homes. These new part-time residents

were attracted to areas that had historically been the least desirable parts of the island—places that were far from the ports and the fertile interior. They wanted the exposed bluffs and cliffs, the promontories, the outwash plains, and the deep forest—in essence, the more remote the better.

The architects who built these first contemporary houses in the 1960s examined the island's existing architecture, either consciously or subconsciously, and combined those influences with their own ideas to create striking designs for the new summer residents.

Three projects that broke the traditional mold were built in Chilmark, the most liberal town, which was also remote and undeveloped. The three architects, whose designs were harbingers in terms of innovation within a vernacular, were Eliot Noyes, Hugh Jacobsen, and Chet Wisniewski. Eliot Noyes built a home for himself that, like early vernacular architecture, is unpretentious and stormproof. Unlike the early homes with their few small windows, Noyes's house appears dissected with a wall of glass. When completed, the design was deemed "a half house" by local Chilmark residents.

Hugh Jacobsen's Chilmark design still appears contemporary, even though it is over forty years old. To make the house sympathetic to its neighbors and its site, Jacobsen broke down the scale into smaller, interlocking components. The result is vaguely reminiscent of the small, clustered structures in the fishing village of Menemsha. This environment-appropriate approach is followed by many of the houses featured in this book.

Down the road from the Noyes House is the home of Chet Wisniewski, which he designed in the mid-1960s and still inhabits. Drawing on New England frugality, Wisniewski fabricated all of the structural components of his home off-site, then cost-effectively bolted them together on the island. Unlike the traditionally buttoned-up architecture of New England, Wisniewski's house is designed for the warm summer months and makes extensive use of glazing, with deep overhangs for solar protection.

The three aforementioned homes, as well as the best of those featured in this book, are not the standard for island architecture. A preponderance of respectful, traditional shingled and clapboard Cape-style homes and cottages

dot the island. For a land mass of only approximately one hundred square miles, however, there is an exceptionally high proportion of architecturally significant homes tucked away from the well-traveled roads. Perhaps only the Hamptons can rival Martha's Vineyard in terms of the concentration of architecturally distinctive houses.

While all of the homes featured in these pages are different, a number of common themes are worth highlighting.

- As is the case with many of the new houses on the island, the projects in this book have been built as second (or third) homes for people who live off-island. In many instances, the architects are also based off-island. In spite of that, or perhaps because of it, the houses are all intensely site-specific and sympathetic to their environment. Sometimes, as in Robert Stern's Chilmark Residence, the references are historical; other times, as in Adam Kalkin's house in Aquinnah, the references are more idiosyncratic but still of the place. It could be that this view of Martha's Vineyard from a distance (it is an island, after all) is a large part of what makes it so desirable— something apart for our everyday lives and therefore more special.

- While most of the island's traditional architecture from the eighteenth, nineteenth, and early twentieth centuries consisted of very tight, inward-looking structures, the houses featured in this book make every effort to blur the distinctions between indoors and outdoors. This is not surprising, given that most of the projects are designed specifically for summer living. The innovation also speaks to seductive qualities of the Vineyard's many different environments, which allow for such interactive responses.

- Many of the architects whose work appears here chose to break down the scale of their projects into compositions of smaller building components. This approach is particularly effective (and necessary, given the zoning

restrictions) for the two largest houses shown: Centerbrook's 15,000-square-foot Pond House and Hutker Architects' 9,300-square-foot Slough Cove Estate. This parti can be found in a number of smaller projects as well. The result is houses that work *with* the natural environment, rather than overwhelming it.

- Each project features extremely high quality detailing and construction. While this is to be expected in a book of outstanding houses, the same can be said for much of the island's housing stock. One explanation is that, given the high costs of land, labor, and materials on Martha's Vineyard, extra attention to detail is almost a given. Another possible explanation, embodied by the organic work of the South Mountain Company, is that the strong sense of place permeating the island engenders a high degree of commitment on the part of designers, builders, and owners.

- Finally, all houses are shown in their original state. Very few have changed ownership and none has morphed over time. This may be the nature of second houses, but it also speaks to the notion that the architects got it right the first time.

The houses in the book are presented in chronological order by their respective completion dates. They represent many styles, from traditional to modern, from Cape to Shingle Style, from organic to tectonic. What unites the houses is they all are well designed, well made, and well kept. They are all also sympathetic to their specific environments. They respect the island and establish their own personas.

1. Excerpted from the Vineyard Open Land Foundation, "Looking at the Vineyard," 1973.
2. Excerpted from the *Martha's Vineyard Gazette Online,* 2004.
3. Excerpted from the Martha's Vineyard Chamber of Commerce, *History of the Vineyard,* 2004.

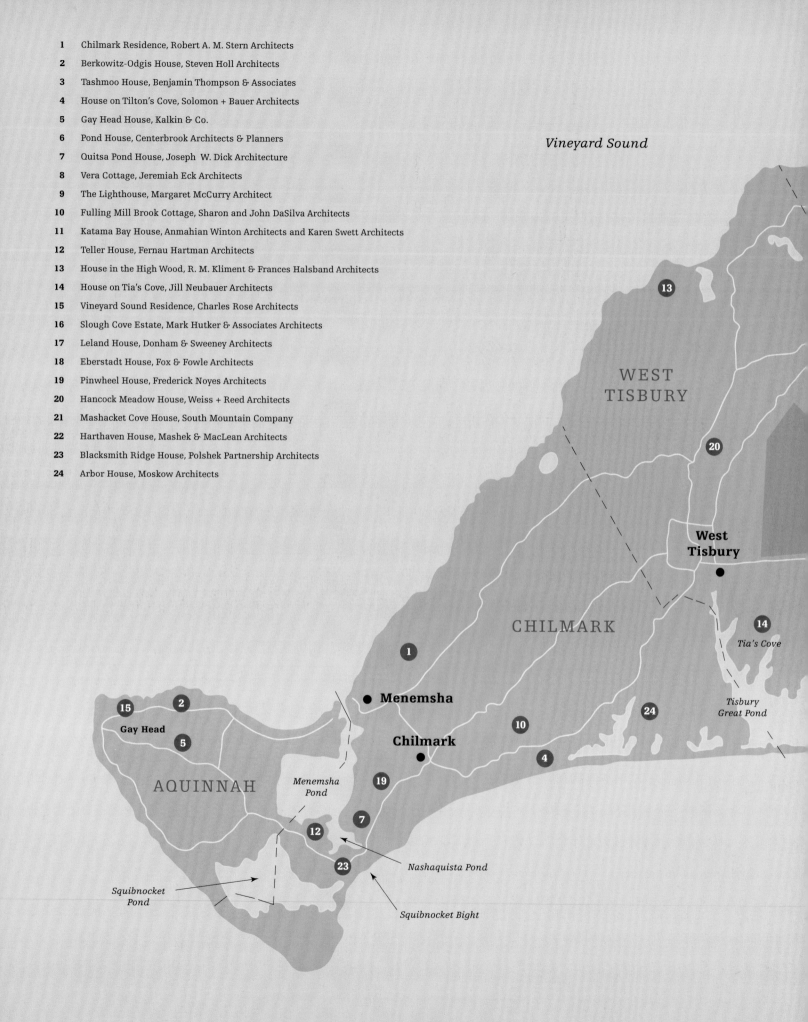

Vineyard Sound

WEST
TISBURY

**West
Tisbury**

CHILMARK

Tia's Cove

Tisbury
Great Pond

● **Menemsha**

● **Chilmark**

Gay Head

AQUINNAH

Menemsha
Pond

Nashaquista Pond

Squibnocket
Pond

Squibnocket Bight

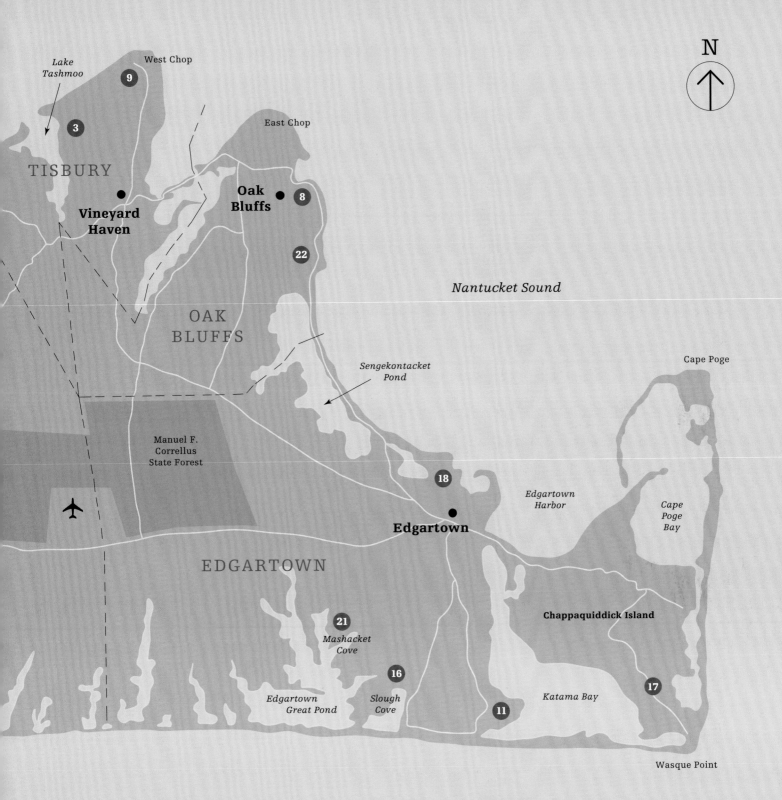

N

Lake Tashmoo

West Chop

9

3

TISBURY

East Chop

Oak Bluffs

8

22

Vineyard Haven

OAK BLUFFS

Nantucket Sound

Cape Poge

Sengekontacket Pond

Manuel F. Corellus State Forest

18

Edgartown Harbor

Cape Poge Bay

Edgartown

EDGARTOWN

Chappaquiddick Island

21

Mashacket Cove

16

17

Edgartown Great Pond

Slough Cove

11

Katama Bay

Wasque Point

ATLANTIC OCEAN

0   5 MILES

Chilmark Residence
Chilmark, 1983
Robert A. M. Stern Architects

Strongly contrasted archetypal and vernacular forms mark the Chilmark Residence. The 3,500-square-foot house faces the sea at Menemsha, the only public place from which the house can be glimpsed, and that at a considerable distance. The visitor approaches the house from the landward side across a crest, and beyond the crest, on axis, encounters a boldly proclaimed pediment suggesting the front facade of a temple punctured by an oversized oculus. The temple allusion is undercut by an asymmetrically placed, recessed entrance. In addition to the house-as-temple design story, the architect also set out to create a modern house reflecting the unconscious vernacular of a simple, timeless way of building. Notable manifestations of this vernacular include the flaring shingle skirting, as well as the square posts that carry the low-pitched, multidormered hipped roof, which seems to float above the porches.

The Chilmark Residence is treated as a long wall, a metaphor for the transition from the everyday world of work and travel to the weekend arcadia of private gardens and scenery. Upon entering the house, one finds that the view is held back by a solid wall that angles to the living room, an expansive low-ceilinged space that focuses the eye both inward to the inglenook and outward to the sea.

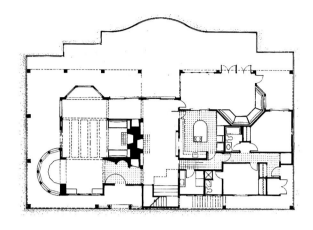

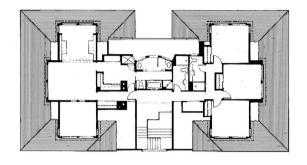

FIRST FLOOR   SECOND FLOOR

Berkowitz–Odgis House
Aquinnah, 1984
Steven Holl Architects

In the locally inspired novel *Moby Dick,* Melville describes an Indian tribe that used to make a unique type of dwelling on the island. Finding a beached whale skeleton, they would pull it up to dry land and stretch skins or bark over it, transforming it into a house. This precedent provided the inspiration for Steven Holl's house, set on a hill overlooking the Atlantic Ocean as it meets Vineyard Sound. To comply with a strict planning code, the 2,800-square-foot house had to be set back from the marshland, as well as from a no-build zone on a hill, and it had to have a one-story elevation when viewed from the beach.

Elevated over the undisturbed natural landscape, the house is like an inside-out balloon frame structure. The wooden "bones" of the frame carry an encircling veranda, which affords several ocean views. Along this porch, the natural vines of the island climb the wooden beams. The ground vine tendrils transform the straight, linear mode of the architecture. The house is clad in wood that has weathered to a natural gray.

The plan is a simple set of rooms set perpendicular to the view within the setback lines of the site. Beginning with a mud and recreation room off the entry, there are two bedrooms, a kitchen, and a dining room in a protective bay. The living room drops down according to the site. The master bedroom on the second level has an exceptional view of the ocean across an exercise area and sundeck on top of the main house.

WEST

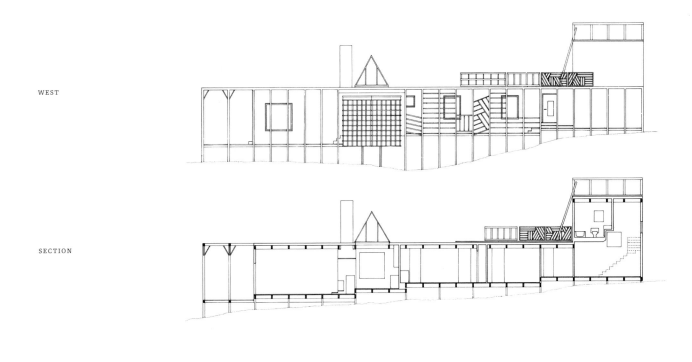

SECTION

SECOND FLOOR

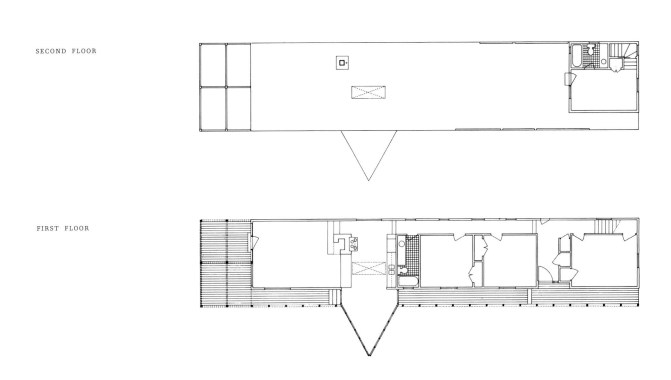

FIRST FLOOR

Tashmoo House
Tisbury, 1985
Benjamin Thompson & Associates

This heavily wooded site has a north view across to Vineyard Sound and Cape Cod. Yet oak and laurel used to obscure any water view until one climbed to the upper branches. The 2,750-square-foot house was specifically sited and designed to emphasize this process of site discovery. The design grew from a careful analysis of, and response to, the site and from a contemporary response to vernacular architecture.

The U-shaped plan comprises the main house L and guest-house wing surrounding a central decked courtyard. This "outdoor living room" is cloistered and sheltered, with a southern aspect making it comfortable and fully usable six to eight months of the year. Covered porches link the two wings while maintaining their independence. The exterior decks nearly double the house footprint, creating a variety of public and private exterior spaces.

The house is woven into the Vineyard's waterside landscape. Selective clearing and the retention of certain specimen trees, including oaks that sprout through the exterior decks, provide shade and screens in the summer months and create a tree-house atmosphere for many rooms. The central living room, with sliding-glass doors on both walls, reinforces the open and informal plan. Capped by a widow's walk, this ridgetop space is just below the treetops and offers panoramic views of the water.

On the interior, exposed wood—cypress, ash, and fir—is offset by simple white walls. The golden hue of these clear finished woods creates a welcoming warmth in the house and a unity with the surrounding landscape. Eyebrow dormer windows surround a loft study at the east end of the living room, forming a captain's deck space for writing and reflection.

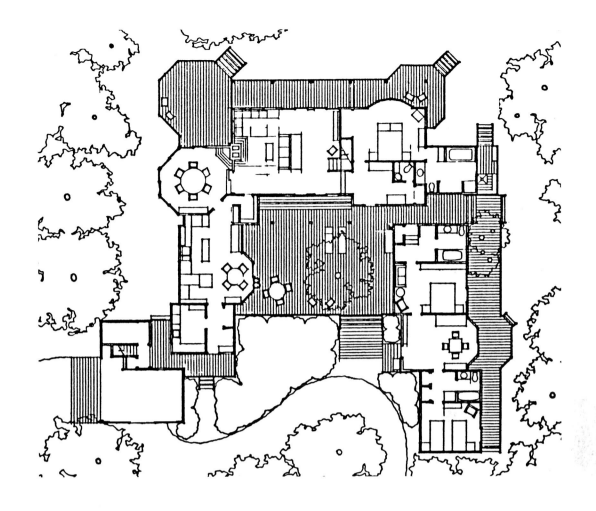

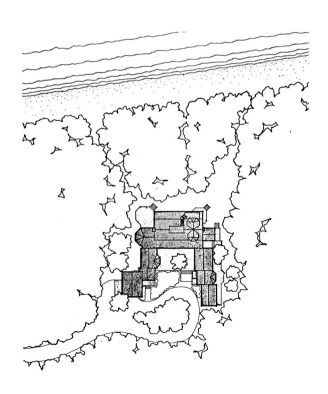

House on Tilton's Cove
Chilmark, 1988
Solomon + Bauer Architects

At first glance, the House on Tilton's Cove resembles a cluster of simple, wood-shingled cottages in a setting of meadows and marshes. However, this is an illusion. Rather than a small village grouping, this is a 3,800-square-foot house designed to enhance, instead of compete with, its natural surroundings.

Set on the highest point of this four-acre site, the house has been positioned to take advantage of surrounding views: rolling meadows, an adjacent pond, dunes, and the Atlantic Ocean beyond. The exterior form responds to zoning criteria, which limit building height to one story. In order to break up the building mass, each major space is housed in a peak-roofed fifteen-by-fifteen-foot module and is connected to adjacent modules by a flat-roofed link.

The design solution responds to programmatic requirements for three distinct zones: the owner's suite, the guest suite, and a central communal space. Three modules make up the owner's suite, which consists of a bedroom, sitting room, office, dressing area, and bathrooms. Within the three modules of the guest suite are two bedrooms, each with its own bath, and a shared sitting room. The third zone includes the entry, as well as the kitchen, dining, and living room in one open space equal to three modules. A freestanding garage with guest suite completes the compound.

Modular clusters are formed around either a small, sheltered deck or a landscaped courtyard. Each has its own exposure to southern, western, or northern light, changing throughout the day and the seasons. The alternating forms provide natural circulation of air and varying views. Triangular glass sections at the raked ends of the modules introduce additional light. Most rooms orient to the unobstructed vista, and all have direct visual access to the adjacent landscape.

Materials used on the exterior are common to the New England vernacular: a wood frame clad in cedar shingles and white-painted wood trim. Interiors are uniformly of white-painted drywall with minimum detailing. Flooring is terra-cotta tile in the public spaces and carpet in the private areas.

From across the pond fronting the property, there is little difference between land that has been developed and land that has been left to its own characteristic growth. The scale and composition of the house, the selection of materials, and the landscaping are in keeping with the Martha's Vineyard tradition.

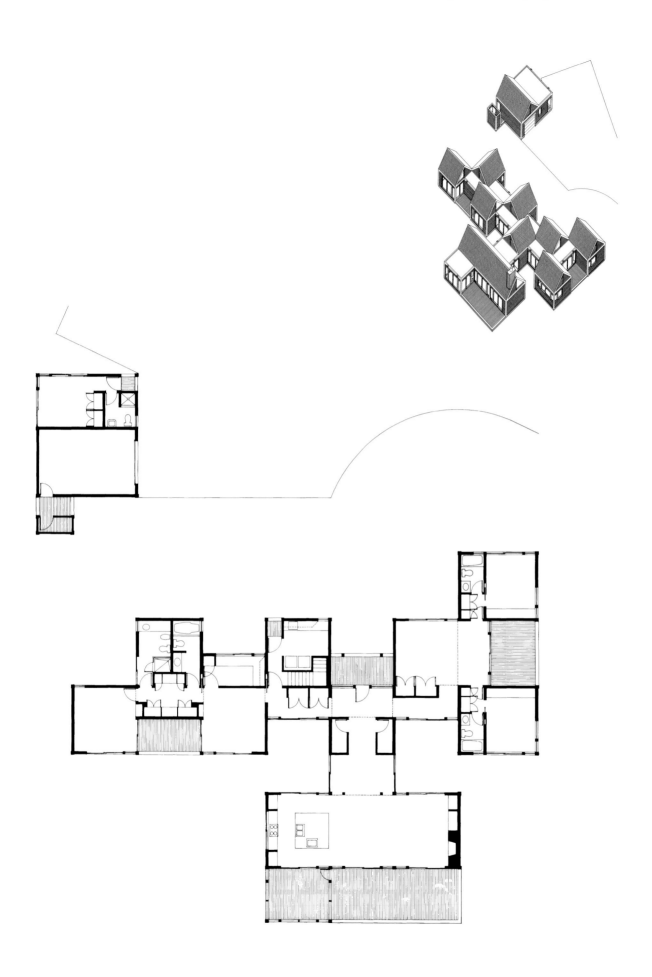

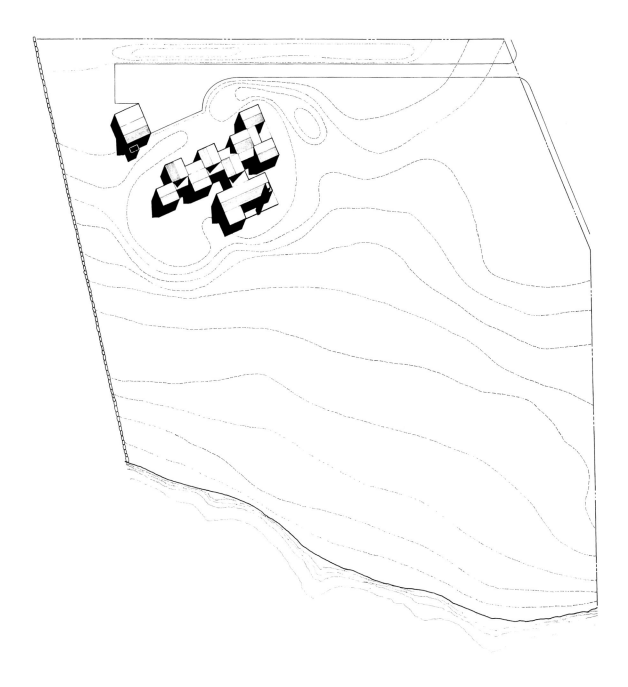

Gay Head House
Aquinnah, 1989
Kalkin & Co.

This 3,500-square-foot house began as a conceptual exercise: in the classified section of a Vermont newspaper, an advertisement for an 1820s wooden barn appeared next to an advertisement for a generic steel warehouse. This accidental pairing became the starting point for a house to be built in Gay Head (now Aquinnah). The town, home to most of the island's native population, is farthest from the regular links to the mainland and has always had a more laid-back quality. This house embodies that feeling.

The architect asked himself, Since architecture often uses a rational language to justify absurd conclusions, why not begin with an absurd premise and try to tame it into a rational experience? So began the journey of assembling buildings of different materials, technologies, and sensibilities in an on-site, in-site performance using only the most perfunctory construction documents. We needn't be patronized by the Modern tendency to make our spaces smooth and our experiences palatable. Some-times a rude architecture can brace the spirit!

Pond House
1992
Centerbrook Architects
& Planners

This summer house for a family of six is a village-like complex of pavilions on a peninsula between a long freshwater pond and marsh. Its 15,000 square feet are spread out to keep the scale intimate, roofs low, and the buildings nestled into a scrub oak forest.

The house is an amalgam of New England architecture. Curved roofs and dormers recall shipwrights' houses. Vertical battening and stickwork that hold large overhanging eaves are reminiscent of Oak Bluffs cottages. The arched windows, which step up and down within the battening, are at once Gothic and modern. Stone is laid in monumental bands in the New England tradition. Inside, narrow painted boards lend a gentle texture to the living-room ceiling and the walls of the dining room, guest living rooms, and master bedroom. Colored plaster warms the domed entry hall.

The buildings arc around an auto court. A central tower there opens below as the main entry, with a glassy study above for one of the clients, a professor. The main house's three pavilions are stitched together by two long hallways. The narrower "Shaker" hall, lined with floor-to-ceiling cabinets, serves the kitchen/family room. The wider hall connecting the public rooms is a gallery. The second-floor bedroom and hall ceilings are animated by curved roofs and dormers. Across the court from the main house are two guest houses, connected by a breezeway and leading to an outdoor pool, protected by a zigzag trellis wall.

The site was kept as natural as possible while still leaving space for outdoor play. Scrub oaks are trimmed to allow for views of the pond and ocean beyond while continuing the forest around the compound. To the north of the main house, the forest opens for a great lawn that leads to a sunken tennis court.

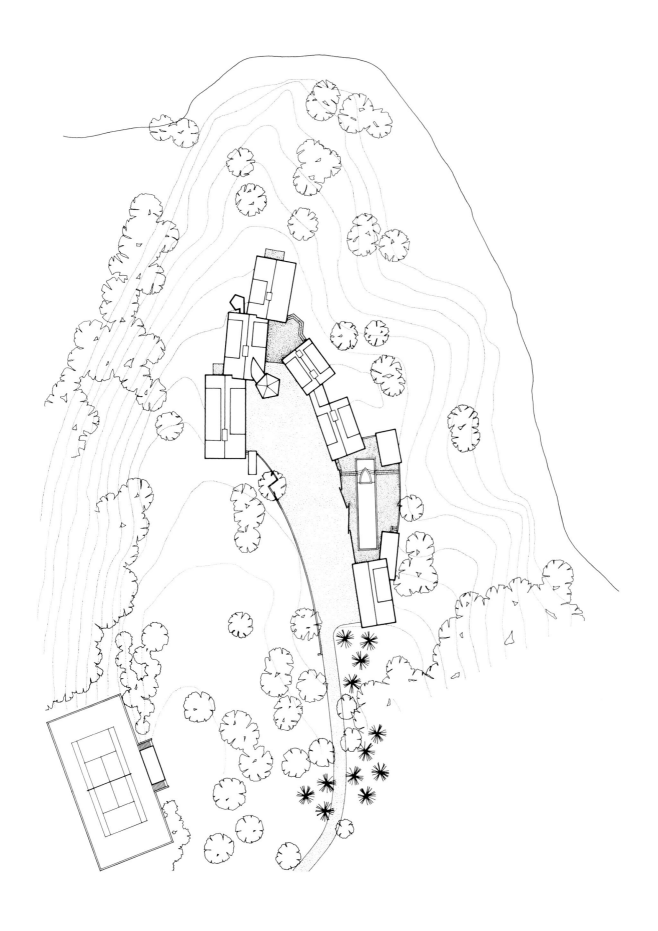

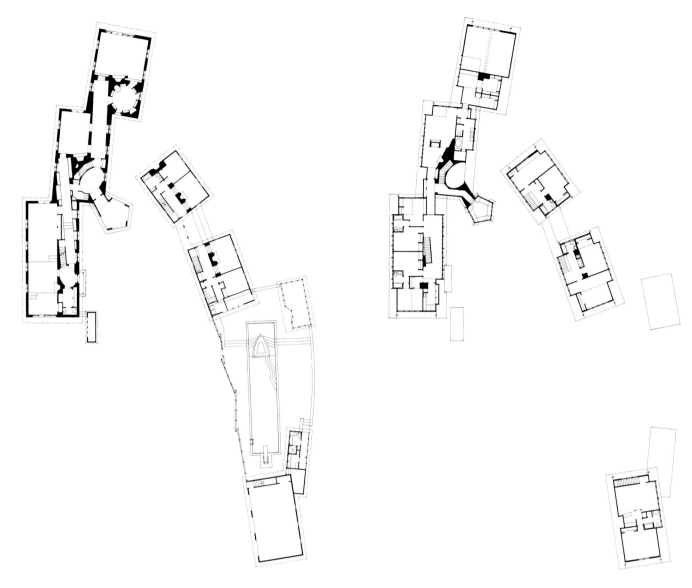

FIRST FLOOR

SECOND FLOOR

Quitsa Pond House
Chilmark, 1993
Joseph W. Dick Architecture

The site is bounded with fieldstone walls that echo the fieldstone used to provide a level plinth for the main floor of the house. The land rolls gently down around the plinth to the shore of Quitsa Pond. The main floor of the 4,500-square-foot house is detailed with a classically derived order of trim elements that frame the views and support the undulating shingle roof. This undulating roof responds to the gently rolling hills of Chilmark beyond and is expressed on the interior as a plank ceiling supported by the ribs of the exposed frame, a conscious reference to a boat's hull. The main rooms look toward the pond and the western hills of Chilmark, and the master bedroom's corner placement includes this expansive view, plus a more intimate view toward the marsh to the northwest. A separate garden room is placed as a pavilion in the landscape and used as an office.

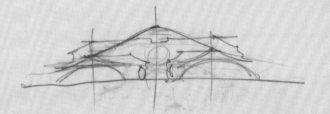

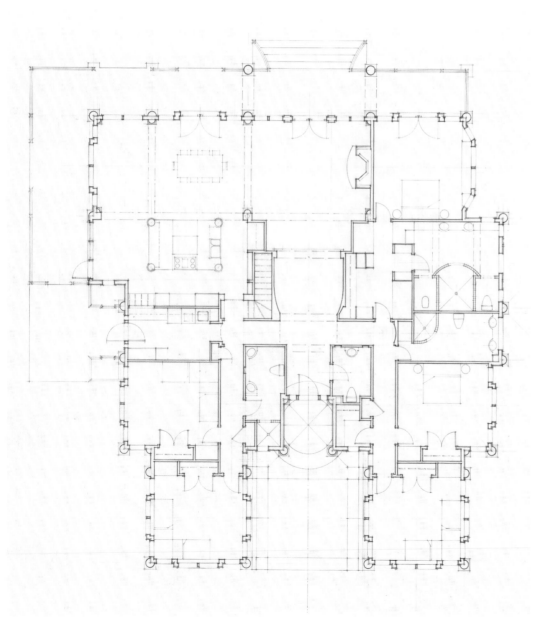

Vera Cottage
Oak Bluffs, 1993
Jeremiah Eck Architects

This 650-square-foot cottage on Ocean Park lies just east of the mid-nineteenth-century Methodist camp meeting ground at Oak Bluffs. Its contemporary Carpenter Gothic interpretation is in deference to both the proximity and the context of those neighbors. In its original format, the Carpenter Gothic style was known for its whimsical forms, elaborate decoration, and craftsmanship. The Vera Cottage borrows some of those forms and decorative qualities but does it in a way that establishes the house as part of both the past and present. For example, board-and-batten siding, an old detail, is executed in a modern material, medium density overlay (MDO) plywood. Translucent glass block is used at the corners, providing more light and spaciousness than a typical small cottage from the past. The hipped gambrel roof also borrows, but does not copy, its form from the neighboring houses, all of which were built in the nineteenth century in a variety of styles generally lumped under the term *Victorian*.

The size of the cottage was predetermined by zoning ordinances, allowing the owners to demolish an existing garage/studio and build a new structure— as long as it conformed to the footprint of the old structure. The resulting plan is quite simple: a combined sitting/dining/kitchen room on the first floor and a single bedroom on the second. Outdoor decks at both levels complement those spaces. The major materials are cedar shingles, battened MDO plywood, and asphalt roof shingles on the exterior, and painted pine wainscoting, exposed pine structural floor joists and decking, cherry cabinets and trim, and glass-block corners on the interior.

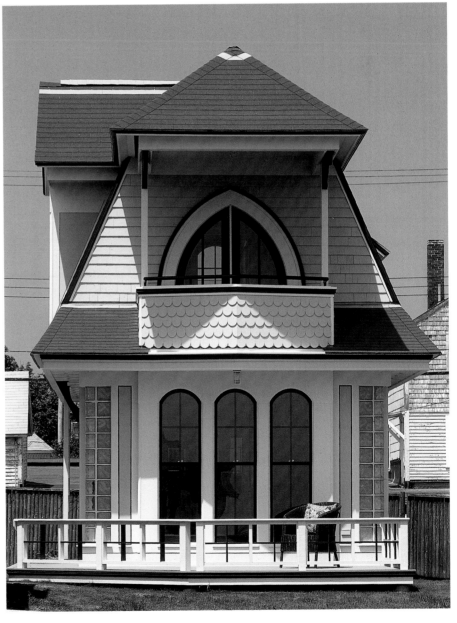

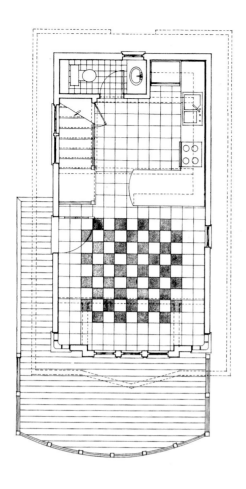

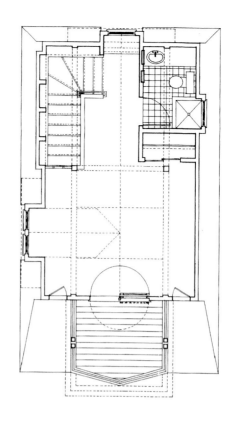

FIRST FLOOR

SECOND FLOOR

The Lighthouse
Vineyard Haven, 1993
Margaret McCurry Architect

The Lighthouse, sited on a wooded acre of land adjacent to the coast, was designed to respect the existing vernacular architecture while establishing its own persona—a personality which reflects that of its owners. Sand and wet bathing suits should not phase it. Breezes should blow through it carrying the sound of bell buoys and the smell of salt air. Sunlight should cross its rooms in summer and fires burn and crumble on its hearths in winter.

A wish list, which helped to shape the design of the 3,000-square-foot residence, consisted of a widow's walk above the roofline, two second-floor bedrooms for the clients' children with play lofts and baths, and two guest bedrooms. The ground floor required a formal entrance and places to assemble—a family room, an outdoor deck, a kitchen—as well as places to withdraw—a master suite and study. These first-floor rooms form an enfilade, a formal progression along parallel axes that, coupled with a symmetrical order, defers to antecedents from other centuries.

A playful lighthouse stair tower became the linchpin of the front facade. The lowest windows of the lighthouse illuminate the basement stair, which is tucked underneath the main stair so that children can run in from outdoors and descend directly. The inflected form of the stair tower is repeated on the rear facade by the bow windows of the breakfast room at one side and the master bedroom seating alcove at the other. The requisite curves also reappear in the treillage that animates this rear facade; its rhythm is echoed by the arched transom windows at either end of the house.

In keeping with coastal New England tradition, weathered white cedar shingles encase the Lighthouse from top to bottom and flow across its inflected curves. The trim and treillage is cedar stained white. The interior, with the exception of oak flooring and a fir kitchen, is all painted a nautical white, which completes the imagery of a stately island residence with a touch of whimsy.

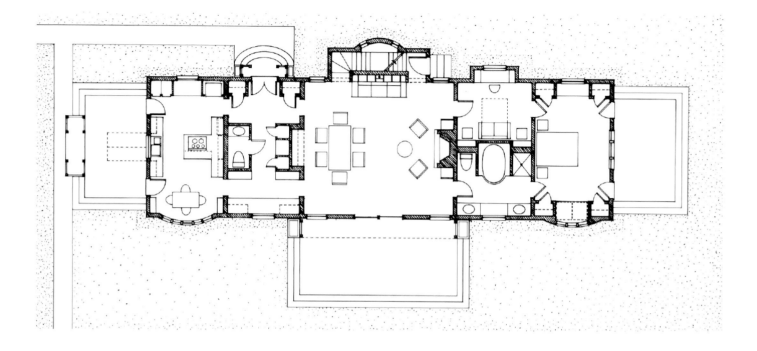

FIRST FLOOR

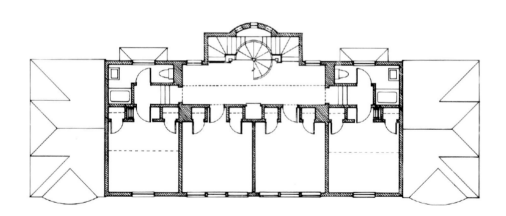

SECOND FLOOR

Fulling Mill Brook Cottage
Chilmark, 1995
Sharon and John DaSilva Architects

With its rolling hills, large trees, ancient stone walls, and rocky brooks, the Fulling Mill section of Chilmark is often compared to rural Vermont. The project site slopes down to brooks bordering the property on two sides. Most of the site is wooded wetlands. A small buildable area at the top of the hill looks out to woods of native oak, maple, and beetlebung trees.

Since first coming to the island, the owners have enjoyed the exuberance of the cottages of Oak Bluffs. The original idea was to build a similar cottage, but the site implied something a little different: it suggested a tree house. Both ideas are combined in the cottage.

The porch, with its curves and brackets, recalls the Victorian Gothic of Oak Bluffs, but the details are flattened and enlarged to be visible from a distance through the trees. When approached from the road, the front of the house is seen through a "cathedral" of trees. Vertical elements in the porch structure and the board-and-batten siding on the adjacent wall echo the scale and verticality of the trees.

Like shoreline houses designed to expand water views, this 950-square-foot cottage has its living spaces on the second floor. In this case, however, the goal is not to create water views, but rather to convey the feeling of being up in the trees. By putting the living area on the second floor, the architects enhance the drama of the space by opening it up into the roof, the height of which was set by a twenty-four-foot limit. A strip of windows that folds around the east, south, and west sides provides treetop views and makes the small living space almost porchlike. Broad overhangs shade the interiors from the summer sun.

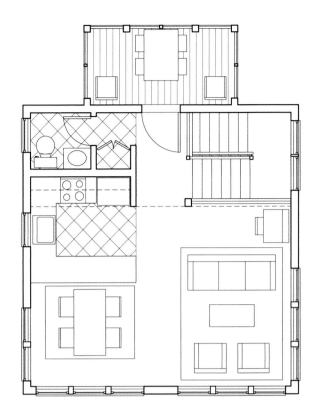

FIRST FLOOR

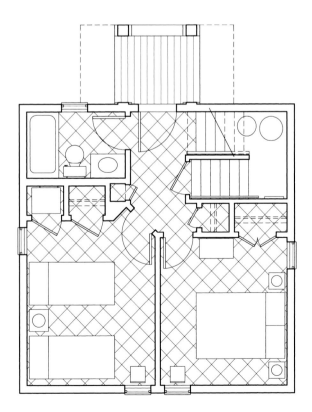

SECOND FLOOR

Sharon and John DaSilva Architects

Katama Bay House
Edgartown, 1997
Anmahian Winton Architects and
Karen Swett Architects

This 4,000-square-foot summer residence for a family of six from Boston sits on a shallow point along Katama Bay, with panoramic views to both South Beach and Edgartown. The site is level and open, yet the visual pleasures of the panorama can be tempered by strong wind and sun. The house is sited to take advantage of the tremendous views, with the primary volume of living space oriented to the bay. Three volumes form the basic L shape of the house, establishing a hierarchy of interior rooms and a sequence of outdoor spaces affording varying levels of exposure and protection. A detached garage anchors the forecourt, which is well protected from the elements. One garage bay functions as an outdoor playroom when the barn doors are opened onto the forecourt.

At the house's core is an open living and dining space. In the living area an extensive band of monumental, awninged windows addresses the bay; when opened, they transform the room into a modern version of the traditional porch. French doors in the dining area open onto the forecourt deck. In good weather the experience is breezy and relaxed, and when the weather turns, the house can be easily and quickly battened down yet still remain transparent.

While weathered shingles and saltbox shapes dominate the island vernacular and provide some context for this design, it is a Shingle Style language of big roofs, broad porches, and scaled spaces that influences the design most. The resulting forms and spaces support the function of the house as a compound where the family can find ample privacy, shelter, and recreation. Bleached western red cedar shingles are the primary material for both roof and walls; reinforcing the prismatic form, mahogany doors, windows, and running trim boost the refinement and longevity of the house.

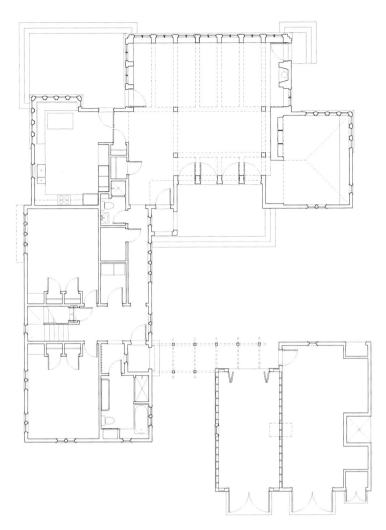

FIRST FLOOR

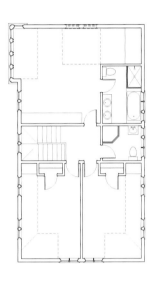

SECOND FLOOR

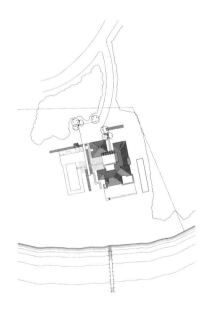

Anmahian Winton Architects and Karen Swett Architects

Teller House
Chilmark, 1997
Fernau Hartman Architects

The Teller House, designed for a film industry couple and their two young sons, sits on a gently sloping, sparsely vegetated site in rural Chilmark, with views of stone-walled fields and saltwater Nashaquitsa Pond. The Atlantic is vaguely visible in the distance, though once-uninterrupted vistas have been altered in recent years by the construction of neighboring houses. The program was deceptively simple: a modest summer house for a creative family, with room for independent and collective pursuits.

The architects and their clients took as their point of departure the local vernacular. Yet in the nearby village of Menemsha, they found the spaces between the buildings even more interesting than the buildings themselves. In the dense confluence of fishing shacks rising above the harbor, complex geometries played with scale, creating forced perspectives and framing views. In these pockets between buildings, architecture became curiously ambiguous, and the traditional quality of the elements was eclipsed by a strange, ultramodern sense of fragmented and compressed space.

Individual structures, too, expressed tradition and innovation in equal measure. This tension between the formulaic and the improvisational gave the local colonial vernacular a collagelike quality.

Working with this notion of collage, architects Fernau and Hartman divided the 2,160-square-foot house into three parts (one for adults, one for children, and one for family) and expressed each part as an independent gabled building. The three gabled pieces come together to shape a large screened porch, the most significant space of the house. As they slice through or are embedded in this central area, the buildings edit and enhance near and distant views. Materials were chosen to help the house recede into the surrounding landscape: cedar shingles, cedar board siding, copper standing seam roofs, copper shingles, mahogany decking, wood, and painted steel.

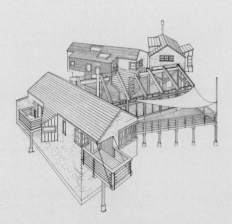

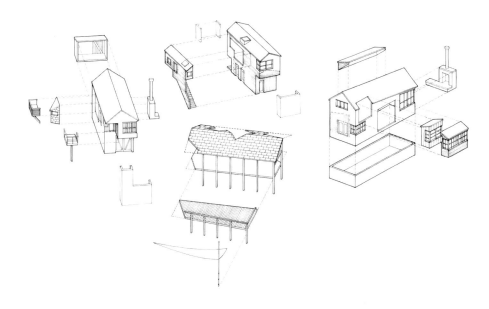

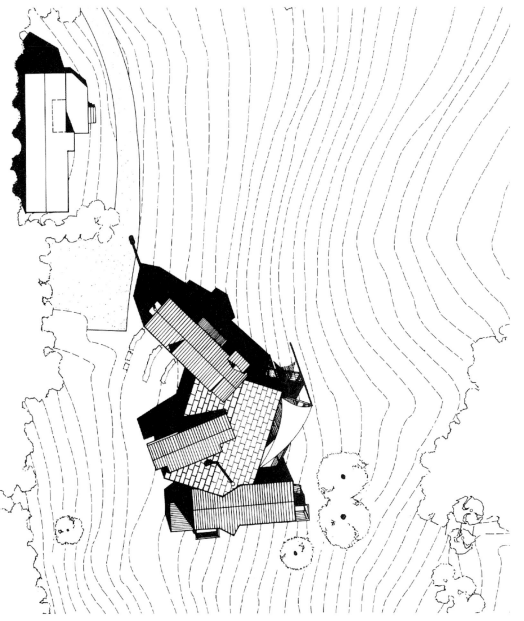

House in the High Wood
West Tisbury, 1997
R. M. Kliment and
Frances Halsband Architects

This year-round vacation house is set on a secluded, wooded slope overlooking the northwest shore of the island. The 3,750-square-foot house is long, narrow, and tall, sited and designed to define and engage two distinct landscapes: one contained by the rising, densely wooded slope to the south; the other open over the treetops to the sea. The garage, sited away from the house, contributes to the definition of the inland space. The rooms are organized in plan and in section in relation to the landscape: to views of the ocean and to the containment of the woods. The stair and the halls are designed in alternating relation to both.

This relationship between the plan and the landscape is reflected in the composition of the elevations. To the south, the entrance elevation is a protective enclosing wall that defines a lawn area, a clearing in the woods. The window openings illuminate private spaces. They are composed to set off the form of the entry porch and the bay window of the stair. In contrast, the north elevation walls dissolve into continuous windows, porches, and decks, opening onto a lawn and garden, with the ocean beyond.

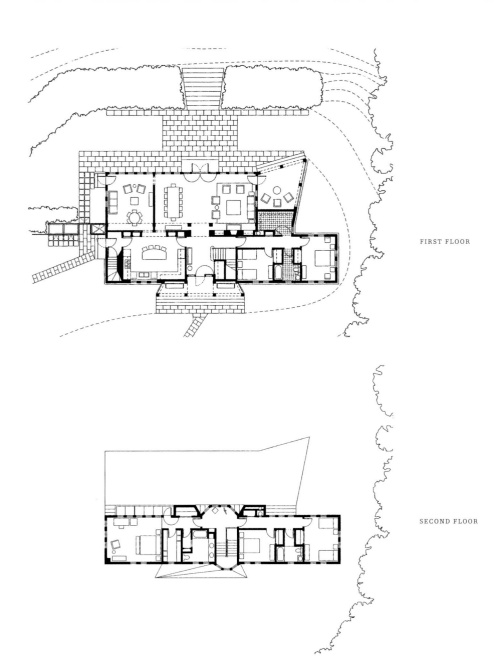

FIRST FLOOR

SECOND FLOOR

House on Tia's Cove
West Tisbury, 1997
Jill Neubauer Architects

In the spring of 1996, Jill Neubauer Architects was hired to design a new 3,800-square-foot vacation home in West Tisbury. The site is a low, sandy forest of scrub oaks and pines with an orientation to the south overlooking the Tia's Cove, on one of the Great Ponds. Access to the site is from the northeast. Using a West Tisbury farmhouse as a precedent for the project, the architect oriented a collection of simple gabled buildings on the site to focus each building toward an engaging view. One's gaze moves from the quiet and plain front facade toward the water and the sunlight. The great room looks over the pond and curving deck. The master and guest bedrooms are oriented toward the ocean beyond, and the office-and-guest-bedroom wing opens to the woodland.

The house glorifies its location on the water and in the pine woodland with imagery of fish, animals, and pine cones, integrated into the building components throughout the house and into the screen pavilion, hot tub, and outdoor shower.

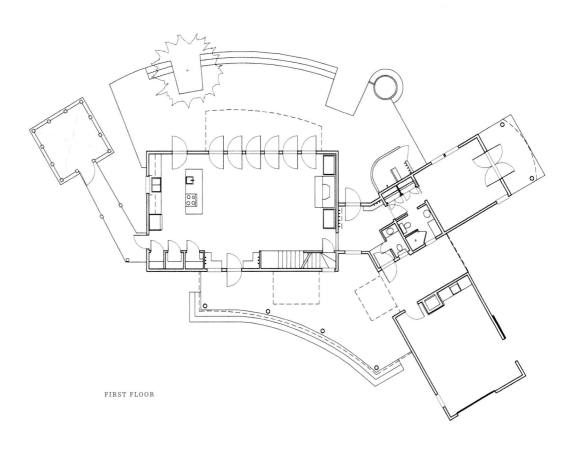

FIRST FLOOR

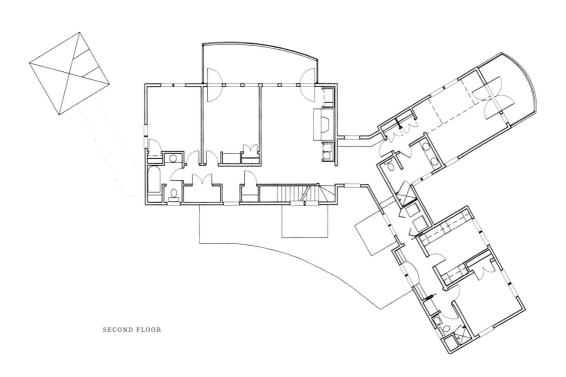

SECOND FLOOR

128

Vineyard Sound Residence
Aquinnah, 2000
Charles Rose Architects

Vineyard Sound Residence is located on the north shore in Aquinnah, on a windswept site overlooking Vineyard Sound. This modest 1,800-square-foot "camp" has small scale and reestablishes a direct connection to the landscape. The design deemphasizes interior space in an attempt to break current Vineyard trends toward larger, suburban-style homes that defy a connection to the landscape, both visually and experientially, and minimize the direct experience of place. This design seeks to recalibrate the actual Vineyard experience and allows for a greater immersion into the landscape.

The house comprises three simple volumes: guest bedrooms, great room, and a master bedroom suite. On the north side, a plane of manicured grass is juxtaposed with the surrounding scrub landscape. From this lawn, the volumes form two framed views to the north of the sound. On the north side of the great room, a terrace overlooks the rolling hills and the sound beyond. The overall floor plan terraces with the landscape, and the terraces offer discrete spatial moments within a larger overall spatial gesture, through the manipulation of the building massing. Strategically placed windows create dynamic visual connections, allowing the landscape to inform the interior spaces of the structures. An accessible roof plane above the great room overcomes a local zoning restriction of thirteen feet and provides a remarkable viewing platform above the landscape.

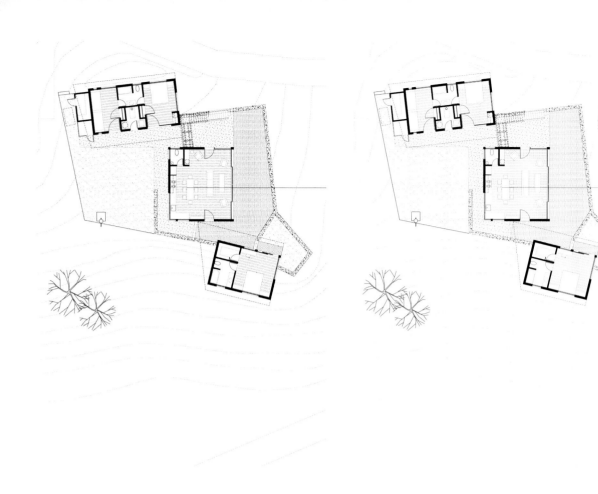

FIRST FLOOR   SECOND FLOOR

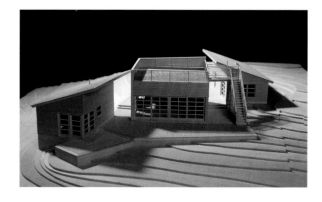

Slough Cove Estate
Edgartown, 2000
Mark Hutker & Associates Architects

Slough Cove Estate is a 9,300-square-foot family compound located on a fourteen-acre farmland site on the Edgartown Great Pond, along Martha's Vineyard's southern shoreline.

To avoid overwhelming the landscape, which is composed of indigenous vegetation, architects Mark Hutker and Charles Orr created a residence composed of a variety of small components.

The house maintains minimum site intervention and uses low-maintenance materials and traditional construction elements. Each component of the residence—main house, guest house, and barn—fits into vernacular forms traditionally found in the architecture of agrarian New England.

The bedrooms are grouped on either side of the living spaces and feature maximum exposure to natural light and views, creating an intimate connection to the land.

Each structure is clad in terms of its function. Lead-coated copper roofs cover the public spaces, while wood shingles cover the private spaces. Inside, rough-hewn stone and hand-cut timbers dominate the open social areas, and a cleanly painted system of millwork, trim, and built-in cabinetry defines the more private living spaces. In addition, large windows capture the surrounding vistas.

Interior and exterior spaces are united through bluestone paving that originates in the landscape and is used to fill transitional spaces between structures. Ground-floor views are maximized through the use of plinths that elevate the living areas by three feet.

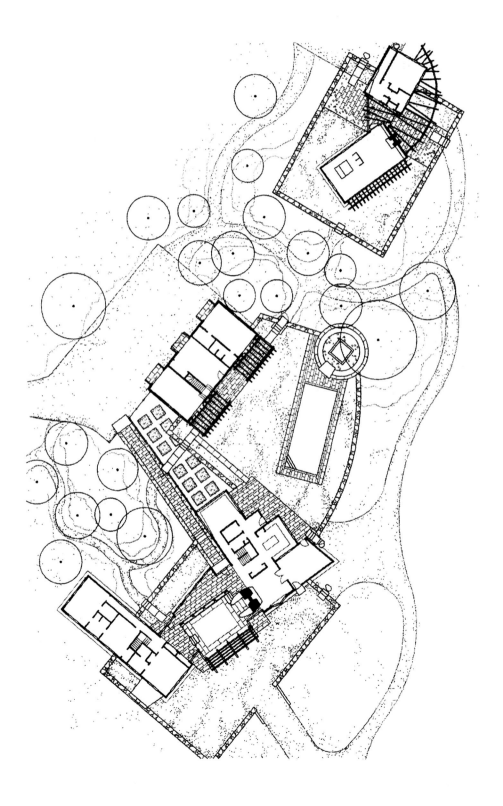

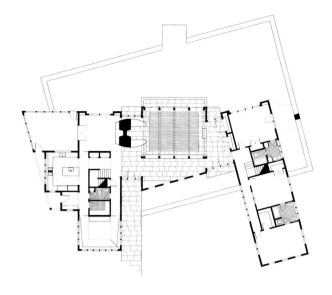

FIRST FLOOR, Main House

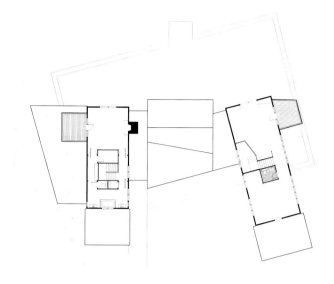

SECOND FLOOR, Main House

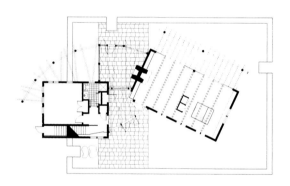

FIRST FLOOR, Small House

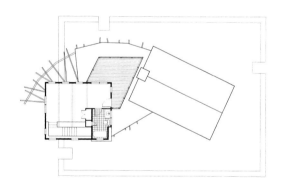

SECOND FLOOR, Small House

Leland House
Chappaquiddick, 2001
Donham & Sweeney Architects

The eastern arm of Martha's Vineyard is a separate island, Chappaquiddick. At its eastern edge is a landscape of gently undulating moors covered with bearberry, wild grasses, bayberry bushes, and clumps of pitch pine and cedar trees. In hollows, somewhat protected from the wind, are twisted, stunted, but ancient oak trees. Kettle holes hold freshwater. Marshes and shallow saltwater inlets line the shore. Running north-south for five miles is a spectacular sand beach beyond which is the open Atlantic Ocean.

In colonial times the land was used for grazing sheep. In the late nineteenth and early twentieth centuries, the area was essentially abandoned except for a few farms and hunting camps near the water. Hunting waterfowl was a significant fall and winter activity for gentlemen from Boston and other eastern cities. Some locals made a part-time living as guides.

Leland House emerged from this history and this distinctive landscape. The family had kept a duck-hunting camp on the property for sixty years. When they decided to build, there was no question but that it should be a modest house. Its roof would not extend above the treetops of the copse in which it was to be built. The oversized and ostentatious houses going up on the island were anathema to the family, contradicting everything they valued about the Vineyard.

The generating form of the house is a square, with hipped roofs, topped with a glazed widow's walk with its own hipped roof. This simple form was then added to and subtracted from to provide some variety within the "system" and to accommodate program desires such as decks and unshaded windows. The 3,000-square-foot house is clad entirely in weathered shingles in the traditional manner: white cedar on the walls, which turns a silvery gray in the salt air, and red cedar for the roof, which turns a much darker gray.

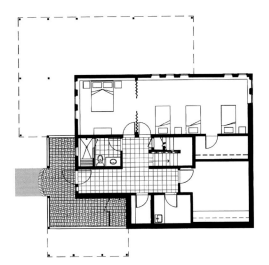

GROUND FLOOR

FIRST FLOOR

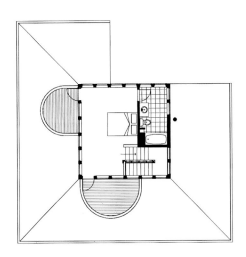

SECOND FLOOR

Eberstadt House
Edgartown, 2002
Fox & Fowle Architects

Overlooking the expansive outer harbor of Edgartown, this 5,700-square-foot vacation house is designed to take advantage of commanding water views. Bruce Fowle designed the original house for the Eberstadts in 1977. The center-hall plan and classic roof lines complement nearby colonial neighbors, while the house's contemporary styling reinterprets the Shingle Style tradition of late-nineteenth-century seaside architecture.

Set in a gradually sloping and partially wooded meadow close to the open water, the original house is sited on a plinth marked by a stone seawall. Owing to zoning height limitations and the initial narrowness of the half-acre site, the second-floor bedrooms are nestled into the dormered eaves. A guest room is located over the garage and connects to the main house by an elevated walkway running along a central axis and serving as a breezeway/canopy that draws the visitor from the driveway to the main entrance. At the extreme end of the axis that forms the foyer and divides the living room from the dining room, a covered patio fans out to the panoramic view of the harbor.

The fan shape evolves from a fifty-five-degree rotational overlay of the massing that sets up a diagonal orientation for the grand stair, the living-room and master-bedroom fireplaces, the upper and lower patios, and the garage/guest room—thus maximizing views while adding complexity to the minimalist forms.

The clients subsequently purchased the adjacent property to the north and, in 2002, had Fox & Fowle Architects design a new master bedroom/study wing in order to accommodate their extended family. The existing breezeway was expanded and reformed as the entry foyer and glazed gallery connection to the new wing. The two new interlocking volumes are set on the forty-five-degree axis to take advantage of the wider views provided by the additional property while developing a harmonic rhythm with the existing massing.

The interior of the house is lined throughout with traditional knotty pine boards set in varying patterns. The gallery is partially glazed with cast glass that provides some privacy while affording slightly abstracted and animated images of the gardens. The furnishings, mostly modern classics, are refreshingly spare in the historic context of Edgartown.

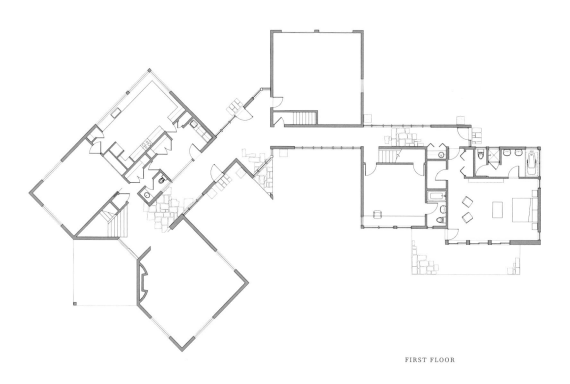

FIRST FLOOR

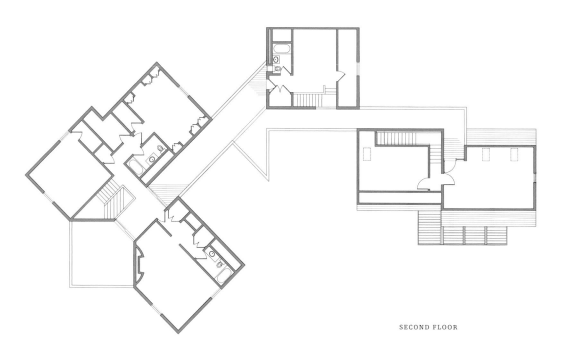

SECOND FLOOR

Pinwheel House
Chilmark, 2002
Frederick Noyes Architects

The clients, retired professors, desired a one-story guest house with a fireplace and ample light. For the present, their children and grandchildren will use it; in the future, they will use it themselves to avoid stairs in the main house.

The design is a pure diagram, a pinwheel set on a six-foot module in both dimensions. The efficiency of the layout allows maximum program in the small allowable area. Details and materials intentionally meld this new house with traditional colonial styles typical of the Vineyard—steep roofs covering smaller volumes, white and red cedar shingles, and white-painted trim.

The eight-hundred-square-foot house is purposefully sited to nestle into the woods and out of view, allowing the natural beauty of the land to remain as unperturbed as possible. Surrounding trees are scrub oaks, kept small by the harsh salt winds, but with long horizontal branches that give a unique mottled light. The house faces the water, visible only when there are no leaves on the trees. Ample glass allows light and cross ventilation in all rooms. Orientation and overhangs eliminate a need for window shades.

The core of the pinwheel is the large, public living/dining space with high ceilings. Surrounding that, the "pins" hold smaller, more private spaces (bedrooms, baths, kitchen), which have lower roofs appropriate to their more intimate uses. Two of the pins are outdoor spaces—a trellised area and a screen porch. Striated light filtering through the trellis mimics the dappled light under the surrounding trees.

As pinwheels can add to themselves in an infinite expansion, the deck is the next large space, the diagrammatic and dimensional equivalent of the living/dining area. The outdoor spaces link with indoor spaces, and smaller spaces open to larger spaces. These overlaps give the house spatial variety and visual contrasts that make it feel much larger than eight hundred square feet.

The house changes character, both inside and out, as the sun moves, as shadows migrate, and as day turns to night.

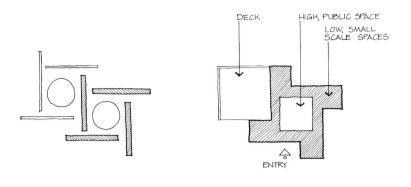

DECK   HIGH, PUBLIC SPACE

LOW, SMALL
SCALE SPACES

ENTRY

LINKED PINWHEELS   HOUSE

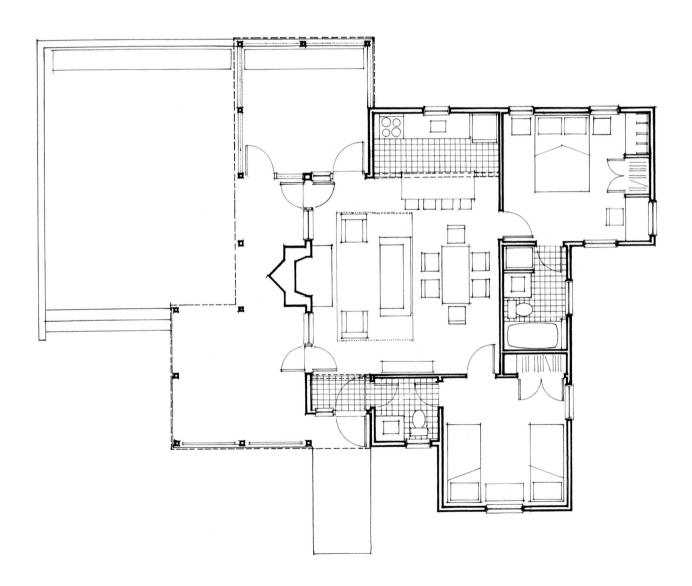

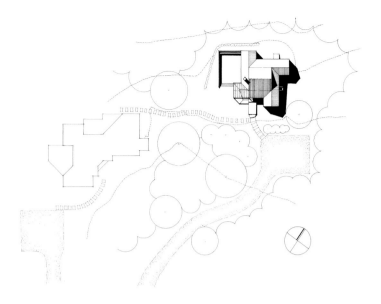

Hancock Meadow House
West Tisbury, 2002
Weiss + Reed Architects

The family's original home, adjacent to this 1.4-acre site, is an unpretentious, inwardly focused, eighteenth-century farmhouse. The existing structure challenged the designer to aim for an architectural integrity and simplicity that could stand up to this survivor from the island's more rugged past.

In spite of barren, open-meadowed vistas from the property, which recalled for the architect the simplicity of the fishing and farming island of the past, it was soon discovered that a myriad of overlapping restrictions had made the small lot nearly unbuildable. After working for over a year with town boards and the Vineyard Conservation Society, the architect was finally given permission to build a house if a design review found it "consistent with the character of the area."

The review board had great difficulty with the flat roof and modern appearance of the 2,370-square-foot house, but after numerous hearings, permission was granted to build to a height limit of fifteen feet.

The architect established a visual and auditory buffer to Old County Road with a stone-bearing wall that encloses the bedrooms at the top of a T-shaped plan. Glazed public spaces in the stem of the T open onto terraces overlooking intimate gardens, a tree-screened wetland, and beyond, expanded views of working pastures, meadows, and distant rolling hills, most of which are under conservation restrictions. An internal stair leads up to a small roof terrace, where residents can enjoy even more distant views as well as a private place for sunbathing.

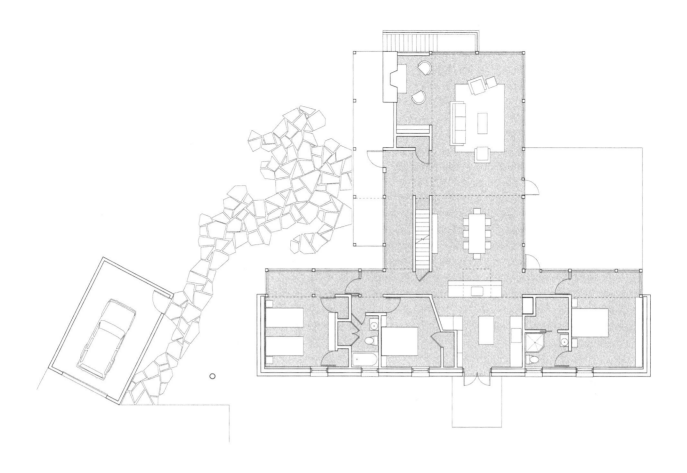

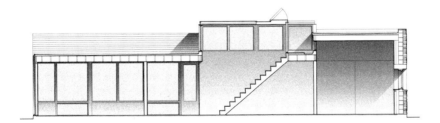

SECTION

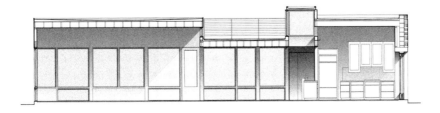

SECTION

Mashacket Cove House
Edgartown, 2003
South Mountain Company

When the regional planning agency denied an application for a golf course on this large property, a series of mutually beneficial collaborations began. The Nature Conservancy purchased the property and looked for a suitable conservation buyer who shared its values. The new owners then hired South Mountain Company to design and build their house. The architects collaborated with Indigo Farm, a site and landscape design/build company, to plan the property, the house, and the landscape. A primary objective was to tread lightly on the land—as lightly as possible.

The site is between the east and west arms of the end of a cove. An existing house was set high on a beam not far from the water. It had a strong sense of vertical mass in a subtle and horizontal landscape; it was poorly placed, and it was not the house the clients wanted. Inquiries led the architects to believe that they could move the existing structure and make it into two houses (for moderate-income affordable housing). More collaboration resulted—with the town of Edgartown, the Island Affordable Housing Fund, and a neighbor. Two good houses came from one, and a new house, more appropriate to the site, took its place.

The new house is a low, horizontal form sited so it deftly balances on the land. It is set back from the pond and far less intrusive than the older house was. The site is planted with woodland shrubs taken directly from the land, so the natural and the man-made merge into a single overall context.

The forms embodied in the house, the land, and the plantings reflect the larger environment— ancient outwash flows and wind-sheared outlines of tree canopies. These resonant forms create a sense of connection with the evolving story of the cove and the surrounding uplands. The L-shaped plan reduces the building mass from the pond and provides a diversity of views from within.

In addition to a quiet presence on the pond and sandy plain, the clients wished to keep their overall ecological footprint small. The architects and their clients decided together to make the house a net energy producer. Exemplary energy efficiency was designed to be coupled with a wind turbine (still in the permitting process at present) capable of satisfying energy demands. Furthermore, the house was assembled around a host of elegant salvage and recycled materials, from river-reclaimed cypress and yellow pine for interior and exterior woodwork, to the massive driftwood arch that crowns the entry, and the gnarly oak-tree shapes harvested directly from the site that support the second floor.

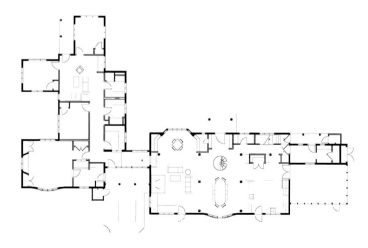

Harthaven House
Oak Bluffs, 2003
Mashek & MacLean Architects

The house is sited at the approximate center of a nearly square, wooded one-acre property. A primary goal in the design of the house and site was to establish privacy and seclusion within a small parcel and to minimize disruption to the existing landscape. To this end, three structures— a 1,500-square-foot house, a 350-square-foot guest house/studio, and a garage—form a three-sided courtyard around a small lawn and perennial garden. The site is cleared only for the structures and courtyard space, preserving the oaks, pines, and blueberry bushes on the perimeter. The septic system is buried beneath the lawn. The courtyard provides a private outdoor space and a focus for the house and studio.

As in the Cottager's Campground in Oak Bluffs, the buildings are organized around the perimeter of a central space. With reference to the colorful Victorian-style cottages in the campground, each structure facing the courtyard has a decorated facade; the battens of the board-and-batten siding, doors, windows, and casings are painted in three shades of red and purple.

While the front of each buildings is textured and colorful, the sides facing the woods are quiet and monochromatic, in deference to the serene landscape. Viewed from outside the courtyard, the dark-stained structures maintain the visual calm of the wooded site.

Each of the structures shares the same building section in width, height, and roof pitch (though the garage is lower) and a common, simplified language of glazed doors and double-hung and awninged windows. The length of each building varies according to program. The simplicity of this approach allows for coherence of form and economy of construction.

The courtyard space is bound by the main house on the north, the guest house/studio on the east and the garage on the west, with the open side of the courtyard to the south. The main house buffers the north winds, the orientation of the guest house/studio minimizes morning shadows in the courtyard, and the garage screens the afternoon sun.

As the courtyard garden is the focal point of the buildings, the dining room is the central focus of the house. The room is characterized by a high ceiling with clerestory windows on the two long sides and a wall of doors facing the courtyard to the south. The low sun warms this space in the winter, and in the summer the porch over the doors provides shade.

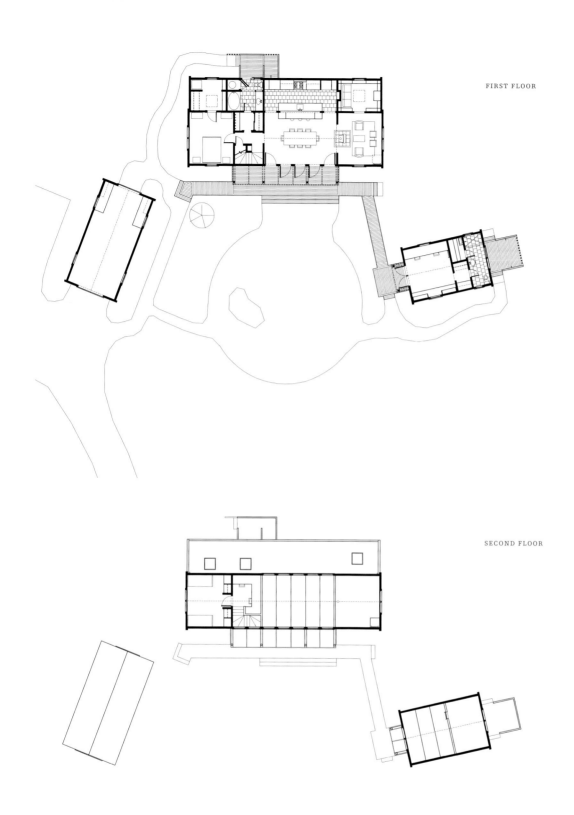

Blacksmith Ridge House
Chilmark, 2003
Polshek Partnership Architects

The clients for the Blacksmith Ridge House requested a residence that was in keeping with the historic vernacular architecture of Cape Cod and the Elizabeth Islands. Characterized by a spare and utilitarian design, these buildings have clean, linear silhouettes and simple gable roofs clad in cedar shingles that turn silver gray in the salt air.

The 4,000-square-foot Blacksmith Ridge House sits on a visible promontory overlooking Squibnocket Bight with expansive views to the south and west. There was considerable discussion about the possible design and its relationship to the landscape. The architects' sensitivity to the pastoral character of Chilmark was heightened by the clients' request that the project's overall massing and silhouette create the impression that the house "has been there for generations." Interestingly, while they asked for a simple and spare design for the exterior of the house, inside, the clients wanted open flowing spaces. In effect, the architects were given a Trojan horse of a program: the exterior was to be unadorned, with references to the historic rural architecture of Martha's Vineyard, while the inside was to be a modern, loftlike space.

The design is a cluster of five cedar-shingled sheds around a landscaped courtyard. Low, unadorned elevations define the approach to the house. The study/guest room and garage form a gate to the protected courtyard, where granite steps descend beneath a delicate, honey locust canopy to the main entrance, leading to the kitchen, dining room, and living room. There, sweeping views are created through decidedly modest openings.

The master bedroom and study/guest bedroom connect to the main building by glazed passages, while the other two structures—the guest bedroom/studio and garage—are freestanding. Inside, the spaces depart from the unassuming exteriors. Rather than massive wood collar beams, stainless-steel cables brace the gabled roofs. Banks of maple windows complement the maple plank flooring. Gray stone slabs and tempered-glass inserts are combined with flush beechwood millwork. Echoing the grassy hills outside, the open platforms of the study and studio descend toward the water.

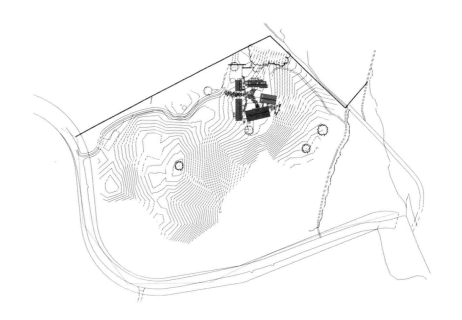

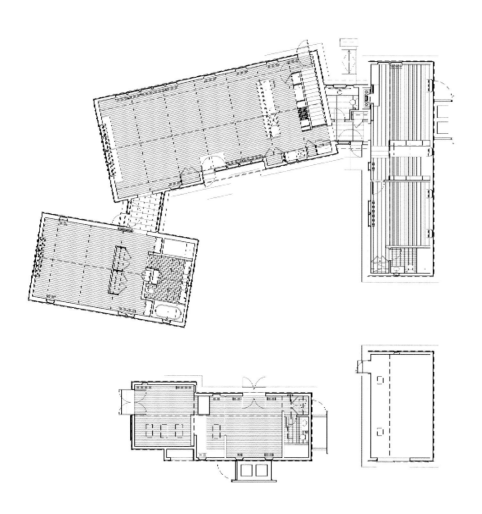

Arbor House
Chilmark, 2004
Moskow Architects

Inspiration for the Arbor House is drawn from island topography and island history. In 1602 explorer Bartholomew Gosnold remarked upon the Vineyard's "incredible store of vines … where they run upon every tree, that we could not go for treading upon them." Many things have changed in the last four hundred years, but the grape vines still flourish.

As the primary feature in this design, the grape arbor intertwines with the house, creating a courtyard. The "outdoor room" expands the eight-hundred-square-foot house by defining exterior space. Within the courtyard, the grass is cropped short. Outside the grape arbor, the natural prairie grass grows wild. The walls of the grape arbor culminate in two sentry towers, protecting and defining the space within. In time, the grape vines will mature and four apricot trees planted in the court will provide fruit and summer shade.

A second inspiration for the arbor enclosure is the seine. Historically, the Wampanoags used such fishing nets, and commercial fishermen continue to ply the Vineyard waters with seines today. In this project, it is buildings, rather than fish, that are caught. In a direct reference, building roofs are sheathed in scalelike, lead-coated copper shingles.

The curvilinear building components refer to the island's ship-building heritage, which is still in evidence today, at the Coastwise Wharf Company in Vineyard Haven. Wooden boats challenge their designers to make the most of limited space. The same is true at Arbor House, where each structure houses multiple activities. The largest oblong component is for living (cooking, eating, working, communing); a second, more linear component is for sleeping and lounging and a third circular component is for bathing.

Designed to be Energy Star–compliant, the house is entirely heated and cooled by passive solar means. Thermal mass and roof overhangs are proportioned in relation to window openings and orientation to allow beneficial heat gain in the winter and cooling in the summer. Two high-efficiency wood-burning stoves, fueled by timber collected on the site, modulate winter temperatures.

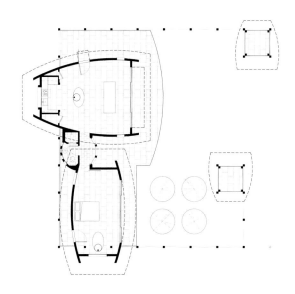

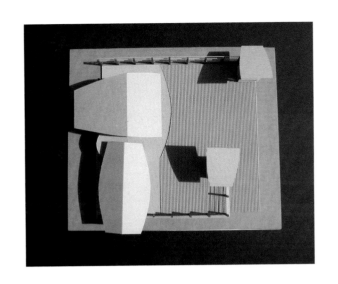

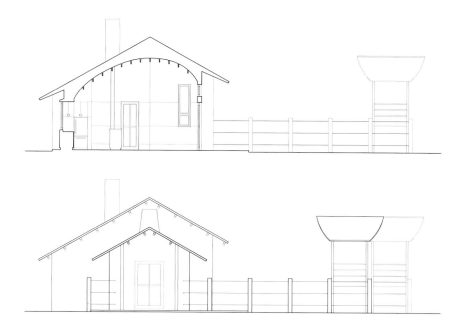

SECTION

WEST ELEVATION

SECTION

SOUTH ELEVATION

PROJECT CREDITS

Chilmark Residence
Robert A. M. Stern Architects
Robert A. M. Stern, FAIA
Roger Seifter, AIA

Berkowitz-Odgis House
Steven Holl Architects
Steven Holl, FAIA
Peter Lynch, AIA

Tashmoo House
Benjamin Thompson & Associates
Benjamin C. Thompson Jr., FAIA
Benjamin T. Wood

House on Tilton's Cove
Solomon + Bauer Architects
Stuart Solomon, FAIA

Gay Head House
Kalkin & Co.

Pond House
Centerbrook Architects & Planners
Mark Simon, FAIA
James C. Childress, FAIA

Quitsa Pond House
Joseph W. Dick Architecture
Joseph W. Dick, AIA

Vera Cottage
Jeremiah Eck Architects

The Lighthouse
Margaret McCurry Architect
Margaret McCurry, FAIA

Fulling Mill Brook Cottage
Sharon and John DaSilva Architects
John R. DaSilva, AIA
Sharon DaSilva

Katama Bay House
Anmahian Winton Architects
and Karen Swett Architect

Teller House
Fernau Hartman Architects
Richard Fernau, FAIA
Laura Hartman, AIA

House in the High Wood
R. M. Kliment & Frances Halsband Architects

House on Tia's Cove
Jill Neubauer Architects
Jill Neubauer
Kathy Joba

Vineyard Sound Residence
Charles Rose Architects
(formerly Thompson and Rose Architects)

Slough Cove Estate
Mark Hutker & Associates Architects
Mark A. Hutker, AIA
Charles E. Orr, AIA

Leland House
Donham & Sweeney Architects
Brett Donham, AIA

Eberstadt House
Fox & Fowle Architects
Bruce S. Fowle, FAIA
Thomas Fox, AIA

Pinwheel House
Frederick Noyes Architects
(formerly Modigliani/Noyes Architects)
Fredrick Noyes, FAIA

Hancock Meadow House
Weiss + Reed Architects
Julian Weiss, AIA

Mashacket Cove House
South Mountain Company

Harthaven House
Mashek & MacLean Architects
Stephanie Mashek, AIA
Kenneth MacLean, AIA

Blacksmith Ridge House
Polshek Partnership Architects
Richard M. Olcott, FAIA
Clay Miller

Arbor House
Moskow Architects
Keith Moskow, AIA
Robert Linn

ACKNOWLEDGMENTS

Thanks to the architects who contributed
photographs of their work and wrote essays
describing their projects for The Houses of Martha's
Vineyard. Without their generosity and ingenious
design, this book would not have been possible.
Also, thanks to my associates Robert Linn, John
Lodge, Newell Gates, and Lindley Shutz who helped
with all aspects of the book. Lastly, my thanks to
the professionals at the Monacelli Press—
Gianfranco Monacelli, Elizabeth Kugler, Andrea
Monfried, and designer Paul Wagner—for making
this book a reality.

ILLUSTRATION CREDITS

Chuck Choi: 132, 134–37, 139
Joseph W. Dick: 68, 70, 71, 72
Craig Dripps: 8, 9, 10
Jeff Goldberg/Esto: 58, 60–63, 66, 67
Anton Grassl: 74, 76–79
Charles Hoot: 178, 180–82, 184–85
Peter Mauss/Esto: 90, 93–97
Charles Mayer: 124, 126, 127, 129–31
Greg Premru: 12 left, 16, 18–19, 21–23, 212, 214–15,
        217–19
Cervin Robinson: 114, 116–21, 123
Steve Rosenthal: 34, 36–38, 40–42, 44, 45, 49
Durston Saylor: 50, 52–57
Samu Studios: 103 bottom, 104 bottom
Peter Vanderwarker: 106, 108–113, 168, 170–73,
        175–77
Brian Vanden Brink: 2, 13 right, 80, 83–89, 140–43,
        146–50, 152–54, 156–58, 160–63, 165–67,
        186, 188–93, 202, 204–5, 207–11
Paul Warchol: 24–28, 30–33
Nick Wheeler: 98, 100–101, 103 top, 104 top

Map of Martha's Vineyard drawn by Moskow
Architects